Author - Robert Juliano

Illustrations – Robert Juliano

Cover (Painting ~ Kassandra) – Robert Juliano

Edited by - NO ONE.

Just done out of pure creativity. Raw, real. Maybe someday I can afford an editor... :)

2014.. As I sit in the "Guided art studio" here in Independence, Oregon. Sipping wine, listening to music.

Do we write this here? I don't know the rules.

Forward

This book is designed to show you how I start the creative process. *Morning Power Talk* – started when I owned a direct sales business in 1997. My job was to motivate, stimulate, educate and activate all salespeople within my organization. It was a very fast pace business that required creative sales and open minds. To remove the previous day memories of hearing more no's than yes's. Like a forest of objections, we had to resharpen our axes to chop down those trees in our minds.

You will read how abstract the conversation starts as the mission is to make as little sense as possible, as long as you can. My sales people would use this technique every morning to reboot the brain and open the flow of many things. Humor was always the first trigger. Then some type of freedom would be felt afterwords, which made the mind connect to something much greater than we ever could be. This works for ALL creativity. Getting out of our own way.

As you read on you will see how not making sense 'somehow' starts to make sense. Almost impossible to not stop it from coming together. We learn more about ourselves when this happens. I hope you enjoy it. It works..... Now let's get to it!

Morning Power Talk
Rebooting the creative mind, Typos and all.

Good morning easy listening rocks forecasting the whether or not, here we come. Open the window and smell the light reflecting off of Mars as it chases ladybugs from your chipped teeth into the waterfall outside your glove box. Let's have a morning conversation about visuals and make no sense at all.

It comes in a flows something like this.

(L- left brain. --- *R - right brain.* --- N – your nothing)

L - I must clean the dust from my liver and let their be room for the onions in tonight's dinner.

R – I would use apply cider vinegar with a tablespoon of smaller spoons, like a tea poodle amount. laundry clips on the tips of burgundy tuning forks made from flees in a circuit board, diced up nicely with Christmas wrapping paper.

L – Easy for you to say. I've been down Jack's

Dandelion winter cave as it was filled with boiling water and candy canes. Those snow owls sure make you think of the ladybugs glowing in the dark. Lighting matches for the socks hung on burgundy tuning forks. Makes my liver turn into onions every time I think of spotted owls cooking eggs on river rocks in a dried Arizona riverbed. It is so lumpy and jello like. Have you ever had a sliver in your paradox?

R- I don't remember even if I became the only member. I did own the coat though. It wouldn't... Or should I say shouldn't, do the couldn't paradoxically speaking cemented into my left foot.

L – Why the left foot?

R – Because tuna was put into my spinach custard cream filled doughnuts, decapitating the tops off of all capital letters. Bad right foot... BAD!

L – So does that mean we no long have a president?

R – We are getting Waaaay off the subway, ejection.

Come back to the surface with me and take that periscope out of those glass trees so the figs can grow naturally on the clouds above Saturn. The President doesn't care. He eats honey badgers.

L – Well Double Rainbow me! I'm just trying to LOL the BFF into BRB. Can't you see that my eyes are filled with the constantly? I think not, there for I am... Over there and not here. When's the last time you had tuna filled doughnuts in General Custard's elite diaper. It's a conspiracy I tell you. He lied to all his peeps about the WTF in the chocolate truck. Star buckle up Americano... It's gonna get Johnny Cash out there today. Twist of lime sprinkle toast. Huckleberry is what you'll bee buzzing around the GMO robots, and not the real ones made by humans who never ask what is about them. What is behind their minds that never speaks but listens to the small voice in their heads they call them... But isn't.

R – I think the robots come from the book of faces. They can fake the making of cakes padding flours for doors that open the whores dirty pours in geometric cubical storms. Raining rubik's cubes shaped like ice trays no one uses anymore. Just push the cup into the slot and watch ice free from the corners of mythologies mouth. Mothballs! Saltine crackers smell like the sultan Sea, that's where they grow any-whore. Did you see the sound of sun-rays crackling and slacking it time for packing majestic baffling minds blowing up nothingness?

N (nothing) – I don't resemble that because I'm not even here. But I am without any definitions. Not even without any definition because... Well, I don't know because I don't know anything. Just am nothing saying Well, I don't know anything. Just am nothing saying Well, I don't know anything *8. These words are here somewhere, but not really at all because all is nothing and nothing is for all, after all... But not before. (* You're IT! Infinity)

L – Hello Nothing N – not here - there. I choose to sip some tea under the rhyming tree because people believe that if it rhymes it's more smarter-er.

N – Here's my best rhyme ever.

_____

_____

_____

_____ . I know, I know... Stop it now, or never. Forever is never not a pleasure together in spaces face with _____ and _____ so honey like. Mafia cars and ballroom stars dancing on the black lake, turning it's inner light on as you become liter in dusty windstorms raining not water.... But nothing forever or never. I AM HERE... Can't you not see? Of course not.... I'm to difficult for the ALL of you like stripes of strings dancing in the piano of space and time, that lives in the nothing.

R – Creative I say. Someone told me that it is my job scientifically to paint confusing pictures in the minds of tiny cells. Let me OUT, let ME OUT! Not by the grin of my chinny chin chin bang bang... That push button. Bubble strum purple oranges on that tree not standing but laying in its roots. Make a slave of it. Chains hanging on kites floating in sky boats of plastic perfumed eyelids they called on a payphone to say.... Nothing. Hello? Ben? Ben Franklin?

N – Hello? I'm not here so don't do anything. Leave a cow after the bees. Have a CowBee day riders of the storm. Into this plural we are born. Like a catastrophic mouse inside a tiny lime. I have no popcorn. Yah... 60's Oregon sound.

R – *Look... L - is asleep-ing punching bag.*

L – I am a bag punching sleep looking at me. You are always the reverse of me as I look in my mirror into another mirror reflecting everything between nothing.

N – Well, hello again. You are aware of me not being here.

R – *Tell me L -... Does 1111x2222= 0..?*

L – Smoke and mirrors the CowBee told me, mathematically quantifying equally pertaining too lipstick houses. Draw it on the walls and hear a mothers needle sow a haystack together making itchy jockstraps. Boxing up glove boxes sending them down rivers that fall. This makes no sense at all to be that angry.

N – But it does make sense in the nothingness of everything forever and ever always expanding and shrinking together plucking strings of time folding without words to explain its definition.

R – *Thank you for your time N.*

L – Yay, thanks buddy.

N - I don't know who you're thanking. I am nothing.

Chapter One
Nothingness

"We are at our best when we connect to our nothingness, says the everything".

My eyes can only see so many colors. My ears can only hear so many tones. My body can feel only a few differences. My nose can smell more that my body feels. My tong can only taste even less. But my mind can make something out of nothing and artificially feel all these things as if it was real. Running video clips in our heads to experience a future which never comes. How does this make decisions, sanity says.

Planet earth has many shapes, many mountains and canyons. Many moods as it is alive. My body being is nothing but a bug crawling on her skin taking in pieces of her being as she is just... Being. Atomically enriched as matter is held together by the unseen energy. All together now, 1, 2, 3... As it all sings suspended in an endless nothingness.

If my body being floated above the planet far enough away. The many shapes of earth would become only round with just a few colors. Farther and farther away it would appear to be just a glowing blue light as I could pass my finger through it.

If my body being, zoomed back into earth, continued into a canyon. Then into a rock and shrunk accordingly, my body being would go into the rock and see plenty of space. If I kept shrinking smaller and smaller I would see an entirely new universe. I would pass through the rock and continue until I saw the very same thing I saw away from earth. The obis of nothingness. I have found my truest position.

Their is an everything equal to the nothing. But why would this matter in your mind as we sit on this third-dimensional shelf. Our minds travel above and below... Beyond the everything. In fear of the nothingness.

As I eat my blueberry pancakes soaked in butter swimming in syrup. Steam rising as the smells blow into the obis and up my nose. I already taste it before it has even entered my mouth. My eyes see this Joyful event has my fingers hold a sticky stainless steel folk with the synapses sparking in the computer called the brain. Like static cling dancing in a blanket. We see a little lightening storm when the lights are off blackened by nothingness. A department in the brain triggers memories of always good associations experienced once again at the breakfast table. Everything coming together perfectly real and raw. No divine spirit is sitting with me as I am pondering these things enjoy pancakes with a side of bacon.

Where do these thoughts come from? And who is the one right now asking this question of; where do these thoughts come from. I know I am the one seeing, tasting, smelling, hearing and feeling this moment eating pancakes. But who is the one thinking about nothingness and everything simultaneously while eating? Even more interesting... Who, or what is noticing all these things.. Their is never an answer.

Every time I look into this area I only feel some kind of amazing. Oops... There it is, and goes again. Who, our what is noticing the some kind of amazing. But every time I ask that the some kind of amazing goes away. Again... Who, our what noticed EVEN THAT! There it is again, that amazing. Noticing it again as it goes away.

Is it just a feeling? Like watching a futuristic movie with mind blowing ideas as something inside of us can relate to? And what mind blowing idea has someone else came up with that blows my mind in the same way? Who was that in the who wrote that, where did it come from?

It comes from a place of love. It comes from our truest freedom. It is the synapses of totality emanating multi-dimensionally through the everything, in the space of nothingness. To create is to get out of our own minds and see this amazing, as we capture the wave and ride it as long as we stop the thinking and just be. The pancakes didn't know any different. It just IS...... The nothingness reveals.

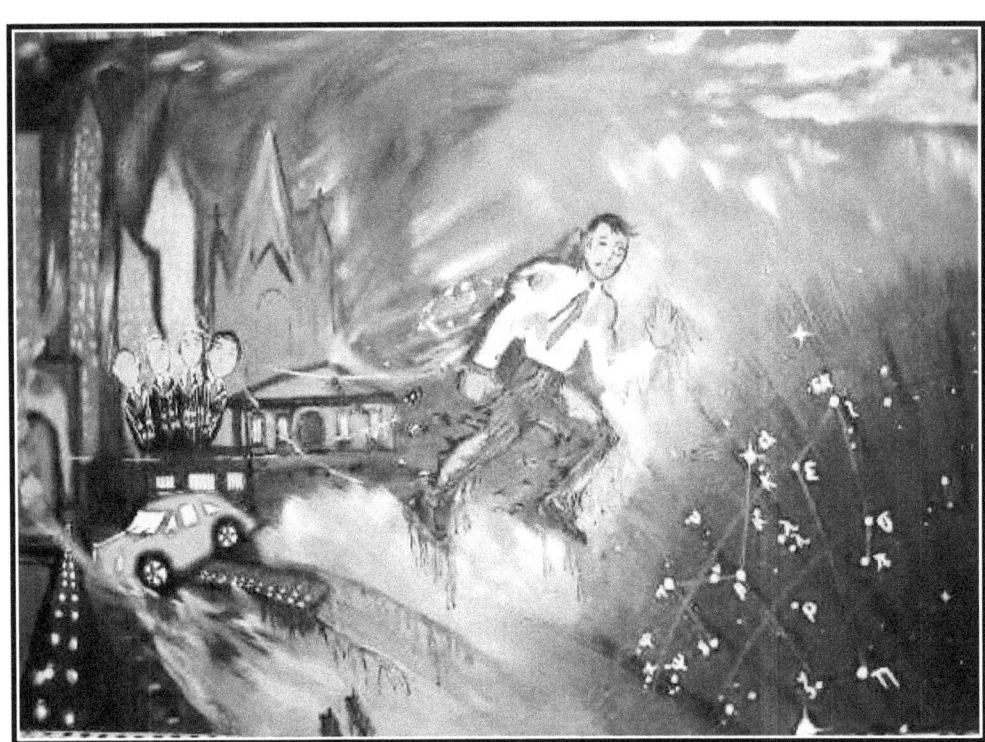

Chapter Two

What about ME?

**"You must pick on the me you think you are,
Until the spoiled baby cries no more".**

Me – Mine, Mine, Mine... Want now is the 4 to B for the me I see in the drink I slap thy face into remission. Put my transmission into second gear and rev it with fear! Fear is my dear I married before this alike – time. Lifetime, the nothing calls it. I see planes, trains and automobiles as the sad Candy we feed me now... And not the BeeCow.

L- Me seems to bee the GMO robot and not the real one. Artificial robots are the worst. They don't really give you the real REAL vitamin pack muscle builder of nobodies nothingness.

R – I was gonna say the same thing as we talk about it openly in the comments on the book of faces. Two BEES or not too BEES... That it is the answer, some smart fella stated from a horses back draped in gold.

N – Why yes... They speared him after shaking his puffy shirt. Drink from the fountain of love for there is no other place. Better yet, he bellowed on his horse draped of gold through the streets of cobblestone. I'll be back! With his metal face red glowing eye, and a built in meter reader issuing parking tickets telepathically disguised as happy thoughts.

Me – Pass the butter and syrup please. I need to drowned my pan and scrub it with cakes. I need, I need, I need... Almost everything. For nothing is not even real so it scares me.

N – But if I am nothing and it scares you. Then where does the scared come from if their was nothing truly to be existing? You must know me better than you think to be at least scared of me.

L – Okay N - . That made to much sense for what we're writing here. Can we get back to nothingness and just visions felt without reasoning?

R – It seems that the more we TRY to make no sense, it will still come to this. ReBOOT time. The ME has done it again. Bad Me! You little baby child of fear.

Me – But, But, Butt... Butte sized Butt. See... I can play as well.

N – BOO!!!! Here I am again.

Me – Thanks.. Now I have to change my General Custard's elite diaper.

L – That happens to be where your syrup is anyways. Disgusting to witness the Me – this way. But you too need and deserve love. For my readers are feeling the Me - being bullied. Isn't in interesting that from somewhere they understand the BeeCows and GMO robots in themselves? And feel for something that isn't even real?

N – Ahh yes... Wasn't that the point? Welcome to the creative reboot. You may now pass stop and go thru.

Hey you, the reader......... BOO!!!!!

Chapter Three

GMO Robots

"Making a machine that makes a machine. Who made the first one. And who is asking in the first place".

GMO Robots (Get More Obsessed).....
They are the most UN-nourishing, UN-nurturing, UN-truthful, UN-satisfying machines made by the UN-alive. Built on a program called DOUBT to create the UN world as of today.

They take the BEES out of life and make them BEEPS and buzzes. They come out of the other end as BeeCows that don't sting. They just modify milk from their but, but, butts.. Butte sized butts as if that's not enough. Robots make the GMO Robots. And humans make the robots that make these things that don't sting anymore. Do you FEEL ME! Nature screams.

The GMO Robot is what we see in everyday people today. It is the last level of understanding. The linear line which floats elaborate rafts always wanting JUST the sunny day not understanding that we need the everything to be alive.

The Robot that builds the GMO Robot is the first stage of awakening. Known has awareness, which seems to require relics of value more acceptable in pawn stores than the trust re-vault in paradigm shifts inward awareness. Yes, these things have many levels. So use your crystals, your crosses, your sandalwood and dream catchers. The next level realizes that these things weren't needed at all.

The humans who make the Robots that make the GMO Robots, is the elite mind using logical awareness only to impress, and suppress better relics of value controlling the nothingness's unpredictability so perfectly divine. For they are the biggest Cowbees who make BeeCows reversing inner identity so you must drink modified milk that only tastes similar thru a simulator and pressed on thru big screen TV.

At which time wisdom will have us question the validity of all these things. All these levels in our video game called - A Life. Who is behind the person who makes Robots that make GMO Robots that produce modified milk for the WHO drinks it? Do you see the loop in this whole. Not spelled wrong...... (Typos and all)

Several levels of not the real REAL, but is all together real because it is ALL the truth. In creativity you get to see that. Relativity creates perfectness unfolding perfectly without your control. Who stops feeding off the GMO Robot's tit.... Get to breath once more. When your mouth is not a suction cup sealed around this great big tit. And after you're done smoking that cigarette. BREATH.................... The Nothing IN. And you become displaced no more.

The GMO Robot is designed to make sense of something that isn't suppose to make sense in the first place. Can you really explain what love is? The only way I have found is to identify everything that 'isn't' of love. Those things are the only things that have words. The truest being of love is the being of love, which has no form, no book, no painting, no music, no movie. It is what's behind all of this. That's the who, or what is being all these mindful levels. And it's their in the first place.... Actually before and after. Can you explain that? But only in our silence.

The GMO Robot is born by the astonishment of nothingness, and here to be seen... But not lived by. Nor is the Robot, Nor is the human. I can't thank you more GMO Robot for what you do as distracting things do. I wouldn't have a point of reference to begin with. So I love you as well.

And that is love.

GMO Robot

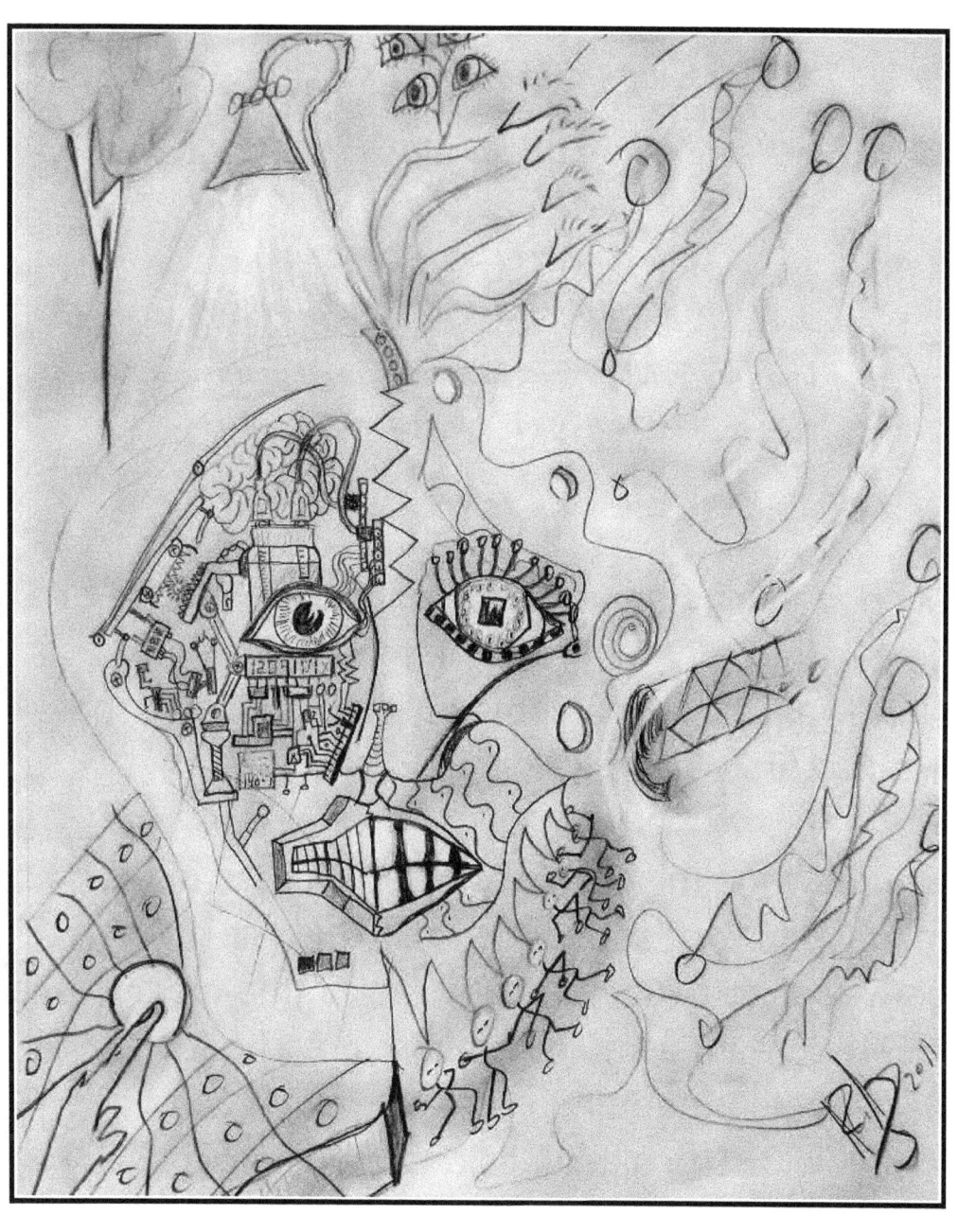

Chapter Four

Living in the mountains, you

have all been lied to.

"Entertainment is never the truth.
The truth is less appealing when watched

in a comfortable seat. Lies are the entertainment,
Real life is much more".

My body being has spent a significant amount of time in the wilderness, in the mountains of the Northwest. My mind comes with it, but it doesn't like it at first. Actually, it never does.

Ooh how the mind whines when planted in the mountains exposed to the raw. This chit chat between the mind and body feeling the elements, a lonely scream as no one is around. The fears believed to be around every tree, at the end of every field. The night falls and monsters eyes glowing all around. The crisp air damply passing thru your clothing. The fires light seems to be the safest place. The mornings, you made it just another night. The food, the water all around. But in the mind it's completely out of sight.

The biggest sales job done to every mind, is this idea of loneliness. I really believe that it is sold and passed on to keep us from discovering what I did. Every movie, every book. Every song, every painting. Markets on the 'idea' of lonely. But that's what makes movies. That's what makes songs. The push in 'not' discovering what you are really alive to see. Their is no such thing as lonely in the truest reality. It is as if something wants us to continue to incarnate the idea that someone is your ticket out of loneliness. But I have met many people married with children... Still lonely.

If they were forced to spend just a few days in the mountains, they would run home to their families and embrace them once again. But in time they will feel lonely once more. Can they not see how the mind dictates the lie? Of course not. They come from a tribe of people called, It's Just Life. Or the, This Is Who I Am people who never question what owns them.

Yes, I remember it well. The first few days was a living hell. But it wasn't the trees, the mountains, the birds or the bears. It wasn't the clouds, the rain, the cold, the snow. It wasn't the fast moving river crashing down trees as I heard them echoing thru a massive canyon. Alone in this huge picture, all by myself. It wasn't the wind at night bring things alive millions of acres all around me. It wasn't the stars barely lighting up the night. Or the full moon bright enough to light up the forest. No human light pollution. It wasn't nature at all.... It was always... just me.

It took me weeks in facing these inner fears. First the animals. Then the weather. I wanted it to all go away. But I was in there home now. These things didn't talk to me, they didn't care. They just did what they did everyday. Some days differently. But it all had a personality. Even the trees were alive with conscious intents. To reach for the sun, to drink the rain water. The old trees washed away from the fast moving river after a rainstorm pounded our everything. They would change the course of direction for this river flowing effortlessly, the path of least resistance. And so did everything in the wilderness.

Weeks would go by and I was still okay. I surrendered more and more each fear as the unknown started to become my home. I knew what everything was doing. But it took hours and hours of meditation. The forest, the mountains wanted nothing from me. It was never impressed with anything I did. It didn't care if I was afraid, all alone as I made almost humans out of trees. They were my neighbors. The birds would get closer and closer with time. I would watch them for hours... I had nothing else to do. The love people have for their house pets was the love I felt for each of these things in the wild. But, I gained the richest fortune beyond the house pet love. I had no humans to compare the difference between unconditional love and the comparisons people have walking their dogs in a dog park. As other people bothered them, and their little dogs too. I felt I was no better or worse, I was in there home.

They speak to you in the most caring ways. Months would go by and everything was still okay. Their was no drama, no emotional suffering. Their was no such thing as loneliness for another person. I didn't want to return, why would I. You have all been lied to about this wilderness. We have been robbed of what was suppose to be.

In the wilderness you live 'presently'. If you lived out of your mind like civilization, you have every reason to be afraid. Their is no place for logical minds in nature. You can't hear what it's saying in every moment for your survivability. Nature talks to you in a different tone. Like the indigenous people already knew. Nature does thing constantly to reveal a direction. You can try to fight it with logical ideas, but you will lose. We have lost the understanding of living in the now and just how kind it always is. Even if a bear comes to visit your camp... It's never personal. It is beautiful and here. And if you pay attention to what is happening in the now. Everything is always okay, EVEN if it isn't ideal. That is the freedom suppressed by the machine of civilization. That IS the very first suffering.

When I came back into the peoples world I felt 'their' loneliness and fears. Despite what their words say, I have learned to read the language of nature. Yes, even in humans. It's actually easier because I am one. You see that almost everything they do is no different than the animals in the woods. To eat, drink, fight, fear. But most of all... Everything humans do is mostly about sex, their is no off season. They wouldn't do 90% of the things they do if it wasn't for sex. And that is one of the biggest lies passed on by the tribe called, 'It's Just Who I Am'. Never thought beyond, why would I take THAT out of my life. I'm not satisfied otherwise with anything else for long. Says the 'It's just Life' tribe so angered if confronted.

I feel the lonely only in civilization. Not mine. Today I do very little with people as it drains me in another ways. I love them all for being here as I am too. So I write these books to carve out my differences so the 'who are you' people don't have me to blame. I have to do what I do says the winning teams that have made competitions of everything. Even love between two people, a competition. Raising children, a competition. Who can appear happier, a competition. Who can know more about their raised religion, a competition. Who can stay out of feeling lonely, a competition.

In nature their is only two competitions. Bear cubs playing. And mating season. The rest is just trying to reach for the sun. You can live for the rest of your life without anyone being around. You would be happier than your mind could imagine. But first, you must confront the lies of your own mind. Otherwise nature, in the wild, will eat you alive.

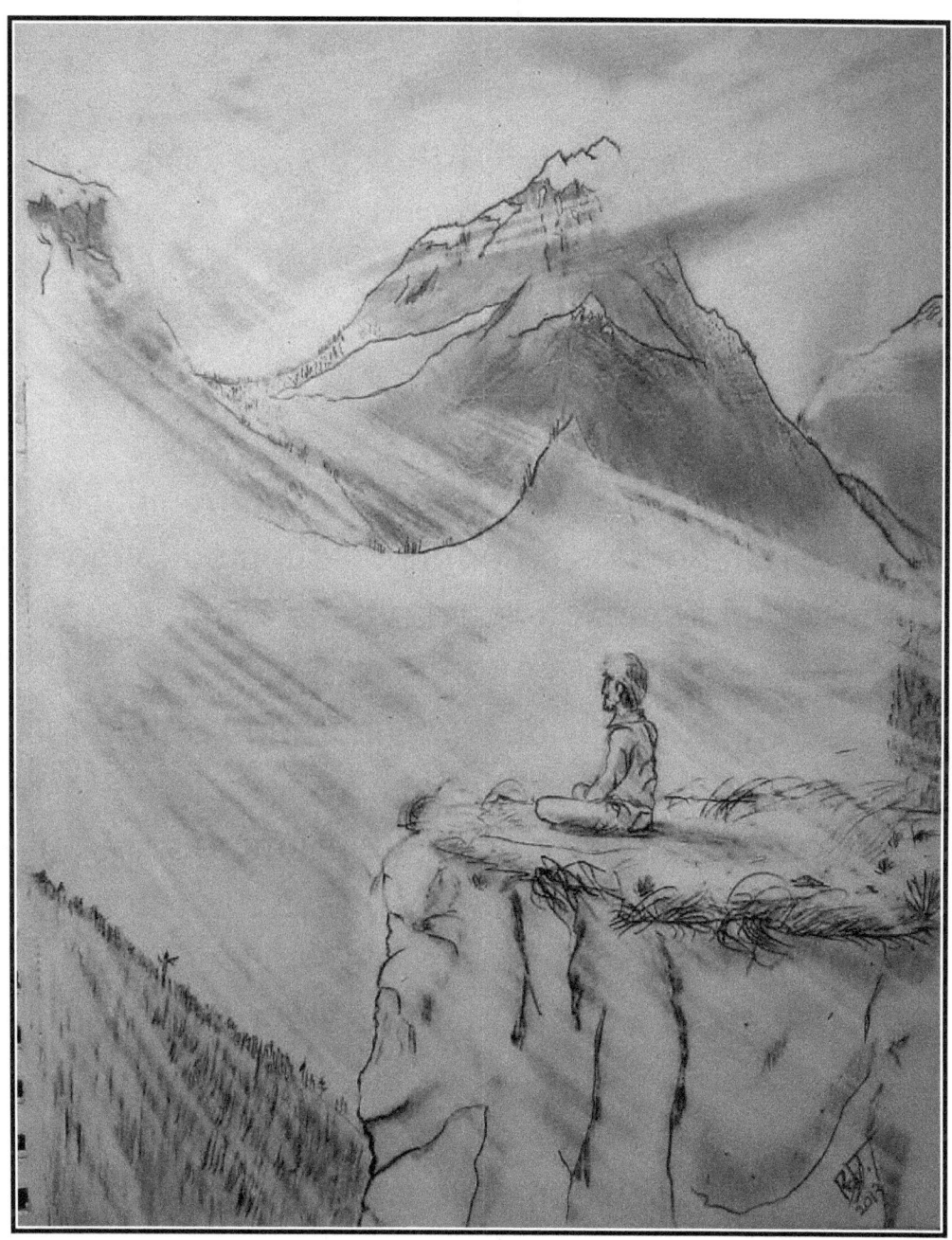

Chapter Five
Connected

"What's amazing is that just now we are learning,
All things are connected".

Vibrations and frequencies. It is communication with everything. It is a communication suspended in the nothingness. It is everything that matters.

Bees are seen individually flying and hunting for gifts to bring home for the hive. To feed the totality as ONE unit connected almost remote control like... But differently. Ants are the same. Birds are the same. Buffalo are the same. Wolves are the same. Plants are are same. People are the same.

As people wanting to win, win, win in everything we try to do. Wisdom will pull that carpet from under your feet several times, until we learn that it is a flying carpet. Whoever realizes this effects the entire hive, and becomes the stronger transmitter. It never stays with anyone indefinitely, not even the queen as she's bloating, but serves a purpose.

True story... I was standing outside talking to someone. As we were chatting away, his eyes became very big looking behind me. I turn my head and saw a huge swarm of bees coming right at us. It looked like one solid mass as they tightly swarmed together. I have never been in this position before. I saw more magic in that than fear. What do we do, I asked this man. Stand still and they will pass.

As they pass right thru us, I felt the breeze from thousands of wings. A loud buzzing noise and the dark cloud of their bodies. I felt BLESSED! And I don't know why. Was it that they trusted me? Was it that I trusted them?

All I know is that abstract moment needed to be written. And maybe painted. Or maybe a song.

Somehow this life speaks in ways we can choose to scientifically explain. But science is just an admitting we don't know what we're talking about... In time it always changes.

In that instant, we were connected closer. But to this day I still feel a connection welcoming me to nature as she wants us all to BE. BEE........ I wont get into the science now understanding the physics of our connection. It spoils the fun. Most of you know it now anyways. Just BELIEVE it. No more DOUBT. Try that on for once. :)

Chapter Six

To conclude. It doesn't take anymore.

"The idea of filling up is never fulfilled. It is ideas that never end, and should be ended when FELT".

Me – I don't seem to stand a chance with you L -, R -, and N -. I thought this was a competition.

L – I am here to make fires, hunt food and cook it. I am here to make BeeCows, GMO Robots and give this world some kind of rationality.

R – I am here to look at the fire and see shapes expressed as feelings. And the food you eat will taste better. BeeCows are the arguments the L – has with me. GMO Robots is the disappointment I NEED to feel creativity again. I am here to question reality. But I am not reality.

N – I am here and can not be understood. But

none of this would ever happen if I didn't exist. You all need a place for your show. What would be before me, nothingness has to be because we couldn't imagine outside, and before everything. So I am needed because that is you... And me.

E - *Everything... I couldn't speak until all these things were realized. I'm sorry it took so many things to the point of nothing. But I love you all... And their are no more words. No more drawings. Only some FEELING.... I am your being equal to nothing. And in my space, you find grace... CONSTANTLY.*

Be here in the middle of nothingness and everything. And your body will no longer be the center of your being. The CORE... Is who you are... In creativity. It is not rational. It is not logic. It is not metal. It is just... BEING. And it will make sense after you discover me.

Thank you.... love you all. *~ Robert Juliano.*

Author

Rob Juliano ~ Is a born artist, philosopher, scientist and story teller. He avoided the arts most of his life, struggling to conform to the standard traditions which did not allow his free-flowing nature to expand. Always 'different', yet learning how to comply, he played the game masterfully until 2007. After a conscious choice to live in the mountains, meditating 4 to 6 hours a day *(eat me bears, eat me cougars, I didn't care!)* ~ then the eyes finally opened...and truth was revealed.

There is a message within every *breath~stroke* that is felt. Every word that is written, by opening up to universal awareness. Nurturing our inner child, once our minds are cleared, rather than living in the static of old, stuffy, reactive conditioning, allows us to truly be free. Within the movement of a new, yet ancient understanding called FAITH, these paintings and writings have a life of their own ~ Nature's Flow. As we evolve and pay attention to the abstract potentiality, it is amazing how a tangible creation brings one to the 'here and now', in trusting their heart.

Looking closely and deeply into each painting, each writing, allows one to feel something organically. This art becomes more profound with time, as wisdom is born. Trusting our intuitive hearts opens us up to Heaven's permission for us to play! The Earth is your reflection...OUR reflection. She is saying today...FEEL from love. Being okay with our uniqueness, returns us to our truest nature. In the NOW, you get to be the authentic yoU!